4-17-16

to: _Amber Lee_

from: _Mom_

OWL ALWAYS LOVE YOU

Published by Sellers Publishing, Inc.
161 John Roberts Road, South Portland, ME 04106
Visit us at www.sellerspublishing.com • E-mail: rsp@rsvp.com

 Like Us on Facebook

Compiled by Robin Haywood

ISBN-13: 978-1-4162-4537-7

Printed and bound in China.

10 9 8 7 6 5 4 3 2 1

Amber Lee,

OWL ALWAYS LOVE YOU

you're forever in my heart...

Art by Debbie Mumm

hank you
for your
eautiful family
So much more
to love!

Love

Mom

SELLERS
PUBLISHING

©Debbie Mu

You are the poem I dream of writing,
the masterpiece I longed to paint.
You are the shining star I reached
for in my ever hopeful quest for life
fulfilled. You are my one and only.
Now with all things, I am blessed.

You are a miracle. There will never be another person like you.

©Debbie Mumm

©Debbie Mu

There are no accidents;
mistakes have not been made.
You have gifts for this world
that no one else brings.

Promise me you'll always remember:
You're braver than you believe,
and stronger than you seem,
and smarter than you think.

—A. A. Milne

©Debbie Mumm

©Debbie Mum

Forgive and give as if it
were your last opportunity.
Love like there's no tomorrow,
and if tomorrow comes,
love again.

—MAX LUCADO

Love is always open arms.
If you close your arms about
love, you will find that you are
left holding only yourself.

—Leo Buscaglia

©Debbie Mi

For every minute you remain angry, you give up sixty seconds of peace of mind.

—Ralph Waldo Emerson

My wish for you is that this life becomes all that you want it to be. I wish that your dreams stay big and your worries remain small. I wish that you never need to carry more than you can hold, and while you're out there getting to where you're going, I hope you find someone who loves you and wants the same things as you.

©Debbie Mumm

©Debbie M

'Tis love that makes
the world go round,
my child.

—CHARLES DICKENS

Be kind whenever possible.
It is always possible.

—THE DALAI LAMA

©Debbie Mumm

©Debbie Mumm

You are a marvel. You are unique. In all the years that have passed there has never been another child like you. Your legs, your arms, your clever fingers, the way you move. You may become a Shakespeare, a Michelangelo, a Beethoven. You have the capacity for anything. Yes, you are a marvel.

—Pablo Casals

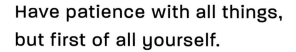

Have patience with all things,
but first of all yourself.

—Saint Francis de Sales

©Debbie Mumm

Doing what you love is
the cornerstone of having
abundance in your life.

—WAYNE DYER

If you have good thoughts,
they will shine out of your face
like sunbeams and you will
always look lovely.

—Roald Dahl

©Debbie Mumm

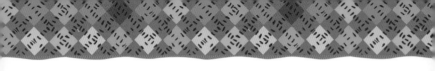

We are the leaves of the same branch, the drops of the same sea, the flowers of the same garden.

—Jean Baptiste Henri Lacordaire

One generation plants the trees;
another gets the shade.

—Chinese Proverb

©Debbie Mumm

©Debbie Mum

Other things may change,
but we start and end
with family.

—Anthony Brandt

I hope you still feel small when you stand beside the ocean. Whenever one door closes, I hope one more opens. Promise me that you'll give faith a fighting chance. And when you get the choice to sit it out or dance, I hope you dance.

—LEE ANN WOMACK

©Debbie Mumm

©Debbie Mumm

Love is not only
the most important ingredient;
it is the *only* ingredient
that really matters.

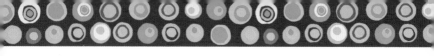

I wish you the strength to face
challenges with confidence,
and the wisdom to choose your
battles carefully. I wish you
adventure on your journey,
and the hope that you will
always stop to help
someone along the way.

©Debbie Mumm

 Remember one thing:
Always surround yourself
with people who love you
and want the best for you.

Being deeply loved by someone gives you strength, while loving someone deeply gives you courage.

—Lao Tzu

©Debbie Mumm

©Debbie Mum

You've gotta dance like
there's nobody watching,
Love like you'll never be hurt,
Sing like there's nobody listening,
And live like it's heaven on earth.

—William W. Purkey

Mix a little foolishness with your serious plans. It is lovely to be silly at the right moment.

—HORACE

©Debbie Mumm

©Debbie Mum

They say a person needs just three things to be truly happy in this world: someone to love, something to do, and something to hope for.

—TOM BODETT

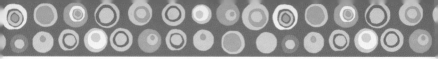

I'll love you forever, I'll like you for always. As long as I'm living, my baby you'll be.

—Robert Munsch

©Debbie Mumm

©Debbie Mur

Be true to yourself.
Love who you are,
and others will love you back.

IRISH BLESSING

May you always have
A sunbeam to warm you,
A moonbeam to charm you,
A sheltering angel,
So nothing can harm you.

©Debbie Mumm

©Debbie Mum

When someone is in your heart,
they're never truly gone. They
can come back to you, even at
unlikely times.

—Mitch Albom

I love you more than there
are stars in the sky and
fish in the sea.

—Nicholas Sparks

©Debbie Mumm

CREDITS

p. 5 unknown; p. 6 unknown; p. 9 unknown; p. 10 A. A. Milne, *Winnie the Pooh*; p. 13, Max Lucado, *Every Day Deserves a Chance: Wake Up to the Gift of 24 Hours*; p. 14 Leo Buscaglia; p. 17 Ralph Waldo Emerson; p. 18 unknown; p. 21 Charles Dickens; p. 14 the Dalai Lama; p. 25 Pablo Caslas; p. 26 Saint Francis de Sales; p. 29 Wayne Dyer; p. 30 Roald Dahl, *The Twits*; p. 33 Jean Baptiste Henri Lacordaire; p. 34 Chinese proverb; p. 37 Anthony Brandt; p. 38 Lee Ann Womack; p. 41 unknown; p. 42 unknown; p. 45 unknown; p. 46 Lao Tzu; p. 49 Willam W. Purkey; p. 50 Horace; p. 53 Tom Bodett; p. 54 Robert Munsch; p. 57 unknown; p. 58 Irish blessing; p. 61 Mitch Albom, *For One More Day*; p. 62 Nicholas Sparks.